Cracking the Code
Making Sense of Daniel and Ezekiel for Today

I moved to Indiana from California a decade ago. It has taken this long for me to find the landmarks and boundaries. Now I know what everything means, but I haven't always understood the local code. When I was told to turn left at Cable Line Road, no one told me that this was an unofficial nickname back when the byways had no names. No one meant for me to get lost. It's just that I didn't understand the code, which was designed to reveal, not conceal.

Major portions of the Bible, including Revelation, Daniel, Ezekiel, Zechariah, and parts of the Gospels and Letters of Paul, are called *apocalyptic literature*. They are often treated as secret codes, which, if stood on end and shaken a bit, will tell us the exact sequence of events that will lead to the establishment of God's kingdom on earth. Video series, books written with a convoluted spaghetti of exegesis, wall charts, and earnest preachers and teachers have striven in recent years to do what two millennia of scholars have failed to do—accurately predict the end of the world and the return of Jesus.

But this is missing the point. The word *apocalypse* means "revelation," and the purpose of a revelation is to reveal. Apocalyptic literature is not written to hide a secret date or place. It's not about predicting the future as we think of it. The only thing the literature is hiding is an attitude, which is being hidden from those in power while revealing important things to the faithful, such as you and me.

According to apocalypticism, everything is backwards: the powerless are more knowledgeable than those in power; the down-and-out are part of the winning side; and the powerful are clueless. Apocalyptic literature confuses many people because they believe in the misguided notion that the apocalyptic message is an inexplicable code, decipherable by only a few sophisticates. That's simply not true. Apocalyptic stories tell

Introduction

the same gospel stories as the rest of the Bible, but they do it in visual, almost video, form, with images coming thick and fast. What matters is the impression formed by all the sound bites when they are put together.

This particular type of literature was written to encourage God's people when they were under persecution or other types of trials. It was written to assure them that God is in control of history. And even though apocalyptic literature may look ahead to the end of time, it is more concerned for the world's present state. God's people are to live by God's rules while they wait for God to redeem history—even when it seems like all hope is lost.

The attitude of apocalypticism is especially hopeful. It encourages us to hang on, to hold on a little longer. The future is coming and everything's going to be okay. God isn't dead. God abides with us. Even when horrible things are happening and it seems as if we've been abandoned, God is with us. God is in control of history. In God's time rescue will come.

The Books of Daniel and Ezekiel are the subject of this Good Ground study. Who was Daniel? He seems to have been a prophet who lived during the time of the Babylonian exile, when God's people, after a history of sin and straying from God's will, were conquered and taken away to a foreign country. There they encountered religious persecution, but they managed to retain their identity as a people and eventually were returned to their homeland.

One of the greatest controversies concerns the date of Daniel's composition. The events are set in the period during and right after the Babylonian exile, but the issues, language, and historical references are more closely related to the persecution of Israel under Antiochus IV Epiphanes ("God revealed"), who ruled Syria from 175–164 B.C., and whose mission was to spread Greek culture throughout the world at the expense of local religions. He wanted his gods to be first, and he attempted to stamp out everything that set our Jewish brothers and sisters apart from their neighbors.
One way of talking about this particular book is to say that it is *about* the events that took place while God's people were suffering great difficulties during the Babylonian exile. But its *purpose* is to apply the experience of the Hebrews in exile to those who were undergoing persecution much later, in the second century before Christ. And that means that the events of both the exile and the second-century persecution are helpful to us in our time of trial as well. The Book of Daniel is a book for all places and all times, not just one place or one time.

Introduction

Ezekiel seems to have lived during the period just before the Babylonian exile. He was a priest of the temple and was taken away to Babylon in the year 598 B.C. Ezekiel's life was a puzzle. He preached judgment and doom until about the year 586 B.C. At that time his message changed to one of salvation and hope.

The rulers of God's people had put their hope in false gods, in their own cunning, or in alliances with foreign powers. All these things failed them. But Ezekiel's hope was not founded on any of the powers of his day; it was built on the power of God. He looked ahead to a restoration of the temple, and even to a time when dry bones would live. Ezekiel, like Daniel, spoke to the present, encouraging the people that God would forgive and would no longer hold the children responsible for the sins of their parents.

Ezekiel uses much of the same bizarre imagery we associate with Daniel and also Revelation in the New Testament. But he didn't just speak of strange things. He acted them out. Ezekiel was a piece of living theater, walking through the streets attracting attention to himself, lying on his side, creating a model of Jerusalem and the siegeworks around it, or holding very still for a very long time. Some have suggested that Ezekiel suffered from grave illnesses, but this never stopped him from proclaiming God's word. In fact, his weaknesses were proof of God's strengths.

People want to be hopeful, but the future looks grim for the world. Atrocious wars flare up around the globe, heinous crimes plague our civilized societies, and environmental degradation threatens to bring Armageddon closer. What kind of God, we ask, allows such things to happen? Apocalyptic literature does not blame God for failing to act or for neglecting to rescue humanity. In the midst of suffering that we bring upon ourselves, apocalyptic literature praises God for being there when humanity has failed.

ABOUT THE WRITER

Frank Ramirez is pastor of Elkhart Valley Church of the Brethren in Indiana. He is also author of the Good Ground study *Choosing Sides: Faithfulness in the Book of Joshua*.

Introduction

Welcome to Good Ground!

Now that you know a little about the topic for this unit, let us introduce you to Good Ground, the series. Good Ground is a unique approach to Bible study. It lets the Bible ask most of the questions and lets participants struggle with the answers. When we ask, "How can I be saved?" the Bible asks, "Whom will you serve?" When we ask, "What will happen to me when I die?" the Bible asks, "What does the Lord require of you?" When we ask, "Whom does God love best?" the Bible asks, "Who is your neighbor?" Good Ground goes to the Scriptures for questions, not just answers.

Here's how each session is structured and what you can expect:

PART I: PREPARATION

We assume that you want to dig into Bible texts enough to do a little reading and thinking between sessions. In this section you are given the Bible passage(s) for the session, a key verse, a summary of the text and the issues it raises, and a three-page study on the text. The section concludes with "Things to think about," which offers some practical applications for everyday living.

We realize that in an age of prepackaged goods and 15-second sound bites, advance preparation may be a challenge. At the same time, we believe that for God's Word to be relevant to us, we need to do what it takes to ready our hearts and minds.

PART II: SESSION

Here we offer tips for your group when it meets, whether at church, in a home, or in some other setting. Good Ground uses a method for study that begins with everyday life (Focus), moves into an examination of what the Bible says (Engage the Text), then suggests life applications (Respond). The Closing wraps up the study in a brief worship experience.

One of the unique features about Good Ground studies is that they tap into a variety of learning styles. Some people learn best through the traditional lecture and discussion, but many others learn through visuals, imagination, poetry, role-playing, and the like. Through these varied learning experiences, Good Ground gets participants involved in the learning, moving beyond the head and into concrete living from the heart.

Part III: Leader Guidelines

We recognize that in many adult groups today, responsibility for leading is passed around within the group—hence the inclusion of notes for the leader in the participant's book. For these sessions to work best, however, those who lead must be prepared ahead of time. This section outlines what materials will be needed for the session, suggests some resources, and offers some tips for making the session come alive. If you are a regular leader of Good Ground, you will likely be aware of our other teaching/leading resources that orient you to our learning philosophy and methods.

Enjoy working with Good Ground as you journey in your faith, growing to be more like Christ!

>Julie Garber, editor
>Byron Rempel-Burkholder, editor
>Ken Hawkley, adult education consultant

Session 1
Apocalypse 101

Part I: Preparation

Bible passages: Ezekiel 38; Daniel 10–11

Key verse: So I will display my greatness and my holiness and make myself known in the eyes of many nations. Then they shall know that I am the LORD (Ezek. 38:23).

Summary: Most people have the impression that the apocalyptic portions of the scriptures are deliberately obscure and that only those with superior knowledge and understanding can decode them. The opposite is true. Apocalyptic documents are written to make it clear to God's people living under oppression that the present tribulations cannot last and that God, despite all appearances, remains active in human history. The message only seems obscure to us because we are not grounded in the historical period in which they were written. Furthermore, North American Christians are not living under the kind of persecution that the ancients endured. Still, how is the apocalyptic message relevant to us in our day?

Study

What do you think about when you think of the end of the world? I think of Vienna Sausages. You know, the little wieners that come from a small can.

The Cold War was raging in the early sixties. We lived on the East Coast. Fears of an atomic war loomed. As students we were required to bring a "survival kit" to school, consisting of a can of Vienna Sausages, a drink, some cookies, and a few other odds and ends. If war began we'd at least have this food to eat in the school basement while the fallout rained about us.

Our family never ate luxuries like Vienna Sausages. We were not poor, but you don't feed a large family out of a small can. So I always won-

Session 1

dered what they would taste like. During the Cuban Missile Crisis I thought I'd finally have a chance to find out, because in those days we lived with the ever present thought that the next world war could start at any moment. But it ain't over 'til it's over. That's the message of both of today's scripture readings from the prophets Ezekiel and Daniel. And that's good news to those who find themselves in a fallout shelter with a useless survival kit.

Chapter 38 of Ezekiel has prompted much interpretation and debate among biblical enthusiasts. It comes right after one of the strongest scriptural messages of hope. In Ezekiel 37 the prophet is taken to the valley of dry bones and learns that with God nothing is impossible and, yes, these bones can live. But suddenly, after this message of hope, the prophet is acquainted with a terrible threat from the north; the ruler Gog, from the land of Magog, intends to invade Israel. In the nick of time, God arises and defeats this terrible conqueror and his army. Their corpses are left for the birds to eat. Swift and terrible will be God's judgment. No one will escape!

> Ezekiel 39:9 also says, "for seven years they will use them [the weapons] for fuel." There are seven years of woodburning of the Magog weapons from this war. Therefore the Magog war with Russia had to be finished in 23 hours in Israel, before sunset, October 4, 1988, so that the woodburning could begin before sunset in order to end by sunset exactly seven years later, Armageddon, October 4, 1995. The World War III date was correct.
>
> — Edgar C. Whisenant, *88 Reasons Why the Rapture Could Be in 1988*

Who is Gog? Where is Magog? Commentators wildly disagree about the modern significance of these ancient names. Magog was one of the nations born of Japheth, one of the three sons of Noah, but this is little help here. There are those who suggest the writer is speaking of Alexander the Great from the fourth century before Christ, or perhaps the Syrian Antiochus Eupator of the second century B.C. In our own time, there have been "scholarly" efforts to identify Magog with an actual nation and Gog with a recognizable ruler of the twentieth century A.D. These identifications have proven wrong in every instance, but that hasn't stopped additional attempts.

In any case, we can assume that Ezekiel's vision always points to a future time, because what was prophesied has not come to pass. No set of circumstances since that time have resulted in the final destruction of God's enemies and the secure establishment of God's kingdom on earth.

Whether or not Ezekiel had a specific ruler in mind when this prophecy was written is immaterial. Over the centuries this description could fit any number of conquerors coming from the far north. The north, in this case, symbolizes no one place in particular, but the edge of the known world, the outer limits of human habitation, and the source of barbarism. The true battle in this passage is between God and those who rely on violence and their own pride, which proves to be no contest. Notice also that this battle is in no way waged by God's people. They are not called to the sword (Ezek. 38:22ff). God can handle it.

The same patterns are seen in Daniel. Daniel's prophecies in chapters ten and eleven seem, on the first reading, to give a detailed timeline, which, if properly deciphered, will be the key to unlocking the end times. Nothing could be further from the truth.

The historical background of these verses revolves around the struggle of God's people against the Seleucid Empire during the second century B.C. From about the time of Alexander the Great through Antiochus IV Epiphanes (who makes an appearance in 11:21 as the "contemptible person on whom royal majesty has not been conferred"), there is roughly a one-to-one correspondence between the symbols of the vision and historical events.

> What is important is not that we should always fear (or hope) about the End but that we should always remember, always take it into account.
>
> —C. S. Lewis, "The World's Last Night"

Some consider this passage to be the most accurate biblical prophecy of all because of the one-to-one correspondence between history and the verse. But in all likelihood, this part of Daniel was written during the time of Antiochus IV Epiphanes and is what we call *prophecy ex eventu* or prophecy written after the fact. In any case, remember, *it doesn't matter*.

Numbers game

As Daniel says, "Happy are those who persevere and attain the thousand three hundred thirty-five days" (12:12), or the "one thousand two hundred ninety days" (12:11). Biblical numbers are not so much concerned with quantity as quality. And the quality of these times are "soon." Both numbers come out to three and a half years, which refers to a broken time, a time cut short and unfulfilled, which is precisely what the faithful desire when suffering under the reign of oppression. The Babylonian year, based on the phases of the moon, was 354 days. The Essenes, a Jewish sect, used a 364-day calendar based on the movement of the sun across the sky, and the Greek world used a calendar of 360 days, combining features of the lunar and solar calendars. All three calendars used special days or months to bring the actual length of the year to 365¼ days: 1290 days is 3½ lunar years; 1335 days is 3½ solar years.

This length of time nearly reflects the length of the persecution of the Jews under Antiochus, but it would be a mistake to take this period of history too literally. Rather, it is representative of all periods of persecution. According to 1 Maccabees, the period between the abomination of desolation, the beginning of pagan sacrifice, and the rededication of the temple was exactly three years. Three years or three and a half years is used symbolically in each case. It is meant to show that the rule of any oppressor will be cut short. This is God's message through God's word to God's people.

> We are currently riding a surge (of speculation about the end time), but this same sort of interest has waxed and waned over the long centuries. And every single calendarizer up to this generation has been proved wrong—dead wrong.
>
> —Vernard Eller, *The Most Revealing Book of the Bible*

Those who see their own times reflected in these verses are right, because the message was the same for those taken away to Babylon as it was for those who suffered under Antiochus or for those who felt the wrath of Nero or Domitian, emperors of Rome. It was also the same for those who were persecuted by religious authorities during the Radical Reformation, as it is for those who suffer for their faith today. It's a message that has been reiterated time and again in apocalyptic literature. Be faithful, be watchful, be patient, be loving. Do not take up the weapons of this world, but resist with love and nonviolence and God will deliver the people in God's time. The mistake is to assume these verses refer to our time or one time only!

The rulers of this world seem so powerful, but each bully finds out there is a bigger bully. Those who live by the sword die by the sword. But those who live by faith in God triumph. Through the examples of its heroes and the words of its visions, the message from Daniel has endured and has given constant encouragement to all Christian generations.

The Book of Daniel was written during an exciting time (Lord, preserve us from exciting times!) when the lifestyle of believers stood them in direct opposition to the world. Some responded to oppression with the sword; some responded by cooperating with the world. But God's message through Daniel is that believers must endure, actively opposing unjust rulers, speaking the truth to power. Believers reject violence but do not reject resistance toward evil. They preach life and salvation. They live in the world yet remain apart from it.

Apocalypse 101

> Rev. William C. Thurman, who, while preaching in Rockingham and Augusta Counties, predicted the world would come to an end in 1868, died a few days ago in the Alms House at Richmond. Shortly before his death he said he had misread the Bible dates and that the end would come in 1917.
>
> —from the obituary of William C. Thurman

If these texts, and others like them, only apply to one specific set of circumstances, then their significance is lost on us. If these stories send a message that is applicable to all times, as is the case with the rest of scripture, then they are beneficial to people in all times.

The seen and the unseen

According to the biblical viewpoint, history consists of two components: that which is seen and that which is unseen. The believer knows that the unseen is more powerful than the seen. We labor against the Adversary with full faith in the eventual outcome, knowing God will re-enter history in a dramatic fashion and bring down the curtain on sin's legacy. But we don't really know the details of how this will come to pass. That's a good thing. We are like students who, if they know the exact day of a major exam, don't bother to study until the last minute; whereas, those students who endure a teacher who gives constant pop quizzes have to stay ready all the time.

Jesus, in answering questions from his disciples about the end times, pointed out that the householder would be ready if he knew when a thief was coming. His parable of the Bridesmaids, half of whom failed to have enough oil for their lamps and thus missed the ceremony they'd been waiting for all day, tells the same message. Better to always be prepared, for no one knows the day or the hour.

Daniel's message, like Ezekiel's, from the beginning to the end, remains the same. Hold on! God is in control! His will shall be done on earth as it is in heaven—in God's time.

Things to think about: What would you and your family do to prepare for the end of the world? Try to save it? Get your affairs in order? Put together a survival kit? What would you include in a survival kit?

Ezekiel talks about the enemies of God's people. Talk with your friends, family, or co-workers about the "enemies" of the gospel today? In what ways are these forces oppressive? How do you respond? How do you think you would respond to political or religious oppression?

Part II: Session

Focus (10 minutes)
After a time of announcements and sharing, choose one of the following options to focus your thinking on the study.

Option A: Distribute boxes of crayons and paper. Draw pictures of heaven, the return of Jesus, or what you imagine the kingdom of God will look like on earth. When you're done, put the picture in a pile and then draw one out, making sure you don't get your own. Take turns telling what you think is going on in the picture you pulled off the stack. After you've speculated on the meaning of the picture, let the artist tell what he or she intended by the drawing. How far apart are the two interpretations?

Option B: In pairs or in groups of three, make a list of items needed for survival kits in case of a catastrophic change in the world. What are the most crucial items? How many are readily available to you? How many could be purchased today if necessary? After two or three minutes, come back together as a large group. Share your lists and make a composite list. Listen as people tell why they believe certain items are essential. Strike off any item that the group does not unanimously think is essential.

Transition: The end of society and the end of the world are topics that periodically emerge in public debate. Some people think they emerge from the cataclysmic stories of the end of the world told in the Bible. On the surface, that's what these stories say, but at a deeper level, they mean something more, something different. Let's look at what Ezekiel and Daniel, specifically, are trying to tell us.

Engage the Text (30 minutes)
Option A: Generalize the apocalyptic story of God to make it apply to all times and places. Divide into two or more groups. In one small group, dream up a fictional nation like Oz, Brigadoon, or Shangri-la. Substitute the fictional nation for Magog in the Ezekiel 38:1-16 story. Also concoct a name for the leader of the fictional nation and substitute it for Gog. Finally, substitute the name of your own country in the twenty-first century for Israel. Choose a reader and practice reading the passage with the group's substitutions.

Group 2 will decide on the forces that work against God's covenant today, such as prejudice, war, or power. Substitute these modern threats for the

Apocalypse 101

word "Magog." Substitute the name of your town for Israel. Choose a reader and practice reading the passage with the group's substitutions.

Come back together as a large group and take turns reciting the passage with the two sets of substitutions. Then discuss the following questions:
1. What part did the faithful of your country or your town play in the passage?
2. Does God's battle against the forces of evil signify the end of the world? Why or why not?
3. Gog and Magog are not an actual person or place. Why do you think Ezekiel prophesied using fictional characters and places?

Option B: The limits of endurance. Examine the two texts for this session. What does Daniel do while God is waging battle against four kings (Dan. 10:1-3)? What does Israel do as God is waging war in Ezekiel 38:14-16? Compare these stories of endurance with the actions of the Israelites in the following passages of duress: Exodus 32; 2 Kings 16:1-4; Jonah 3. Talk together about whether God calls us to endure or whether God calls us to action?

Option C: Get a feel for Daniel and Ezekiel. Look together at the study section of this session or a one-volume commentary to discuss the following questions:
1. When were these books written?
2. What were the big "threats" that Israel had to endure?
3. If these are fictional stories, why do you think they are included in the Bible?
4. Name the times in Israel's history up to the present when they could have used the counsel that Ezekiel and Daniel give in their prophecy. Did they use the counsel? Do we as Christians?

Respond (15 MINUTES)

Option A: Use the following questions to guide discussion about how to apply these passages from Daniel and Ezekiel to our times. Talk about as many of the questions as you have time to discuss.
1. What do you think the world will look like when God's will is done on earth as it is in heaven? How can you bring about at least a little of this in our time?
2. Speak about a great crisis in your life. Were you able to endure until the ending? Could you see an ending at the time?
3. Speak about a time you thought God had abandoned you. Reflecting back on that time, do you think God was truly absent, or was God with

you in your suffering? At the time, what did you hope God would do for you? What happened in reality? Share what you have learned from your experience and how that has prepared you for other crises.
4. From the definition of apocalypticism in the study, would you say it describes the way you look at the world and at God? Why or why not?
5. Many believers look to biblical books like Daniel and Ezekiel to provide a detailed road map to the future. What are your feelings about this? How would you discuss this matter with someone who "calendarizes" the scriptures?
6. Think again of a major crisis in your life. How would you have faced it if you knew ahead of time how long it was going to last?

Option B: Make a list of essentials for survival or look at the list of essentials that was made in the focus activity. Together make a plan to gather the items on the list for one or more relief boxes or care packages. Brings the items to the next session, or gather an offering so that a member of the group can purchase the items. Send the items to your denominational relief program for distribution or to a local food pantry or shelter.

Closing (1 MINUTE)
Pray in unison: Gracious Lord of Time, help us to trust you with the beginnings and endings of all things. Fill us with the resolve to serve you and to allow you to end things on your terms, not ours. Amen.

PART III: LEADER GUIDELINES

Items Needed
Bibles
Chalkboard or newsprint and markers
Paper and crayons for drawing
Commentaries, Bible atlas, Bible concordance
Pens and pencils

Resources
Lederach, Paul. *Daniel* (Believers Church Bible Commentary series). Herald Press, 1994.
Lind, Millard. *Ezekiel* (Believers Church Bible Commentary series), Herald Press, 1996.

Tips for Leading

1. Spend time to visit each time you meet. Catch up on the week, share joys and concerns, discuss upcoming events, and make decisions together. Time is built into the beginning of each session to attend to the business of the group.
2. In preparing to lead this group, read the entire book of Daniel and as much of Ezekiel as you can. Don't worry about commentaries or the right answers or a full understanding of either book. As you read, keep in mind that the message of the apocalyptic books is to encourage God's people to hold on a little longer—together, as a group. Afterward, reflect on what you've read. Jot down questions you have and share them with the group as an introduction to the study.
3. In discussion and study, allow the group some latitude to wander far afield. The action of God's Spirit is powerful; it may take us far from the lesson plan.
4. Use a variety of approaches to study. Discussion questions are provided, as well as more active study exercises. Don't try to do every option. Choose the ones that will be most useful for the individuals in the group and the way they learn.
5. It is not important for the leader to know the answers to discussion questions or to be a Bible expert. The leader's role is to guide participants through the study using the resources provided. The most important role for the leader is to make sure everyone who wishes gets a chance to speak and to make sure that all points of view are respected, even if they differ widely.
6. If you choose Option B in Respond, double-check your assignment and gather "survival" materials to donate to a charitable cause.
7. The leader should take time to either organize a "just desserts" table for Session 2, or make preparations for Option A in Focus for creating a desserts collage.

Session 2
Judge God's Court

PART I: PREPARATION

Bible passages: Ezekiel 16:1-58; 18; 33:10-20

Key verse: Yet you say, "The way of the Lord is not just." O house of Israel, I will judge all of you according to your ways! (Ezek. 33:20).

Summary: Ezekiel tells a parable in which God rescues an orphan from certain death and raises her, only to be betrayed by the child when she grows to be a young woman. The orphan represents Jerusalem, God's people who were rescued only to turn against God later. Ezekiel tells this story to reveal how God's justice system works. Justice is the most prevalent concern in scripture all the way from Adam and Eve and Cain and Abel until the judgment scenes in Revelation. Justice is not just something that happens at the end of time. God wants justice now, for all people. God's justice is perfect, and according to Ezekiel, even God's people stand under judgment. But what does it mean when God judges? Is God's justice a justice of retribution or grace? Is it the fear of God's justice or the promise of it that compels us to be faithful?

Study

Justice. It's the subject of innumerable television shows and movies, both fictional and true to life. In some shows justice is denied and the audience is outraged. In others justice is attained with the capture of a criminal, the overthrow of an evil political system, or with the explosion of buildings, cars, and people. Everyone gets what they deserve. No matter how fantastic some of these shows may be, they remind us how much people thirst for justice. The three passages selected from Ezekiel for this session may seem very different in style and tone, but they are all passages about God's hunger for justice. The surprising thing is that they show in each case that God's standard of justice is different from what we might expect.

Judge God's Court

Ezekiel 16 contains what some call the parable of the Orphan Girl. The story in an *allegory*. In an allegory everything stands for something else. The orphan stands for Jerusalem, and the narrator is God. Ezekiel's narrator tells the touching story of an infant girl abandoned at birth by her parents, and left to die. Infant girls in those days were not prized in all cultures, and some of Israel's neighbors would even expose unwanted female infants to the elements until they were dead.

The narrator takes in this child and raises her as his own. He arrays her sumptuously with marvelous clothes and beautiful jewels. But when she reaches maturity, she repays his gifts with ingratitude, shaming herself and God by becoming a prostitute, using the rich gifts from her adoptive parent to attract "customers." And if this were not enough, she does not receive payment for her prostitution, but pays her customers instead.

> "Let the jury consider their verdict," the King said, for about the twentieth time that day.
> "No, no!" said the Queen. "Sentence first—verdict afterwards."
>
> —Lewis Carroll, *Alice in Wonderland*

Terrible things must come of this. As the parable progresses, the narrator speaks directly to Jerusalem and tells her that she is no better than Samaria and Sodom, two places that have been despised for centuries for their wickedness. A terrible justice will come to all three places, the narrator assures Jerusalem. We can only imagine the plagues, firestorms, lightening bolts, and afflictions God will use to punish unfaithfulness. People in Ezekiel's day were just as scared as we are by this raw, wild parable, with overblown images and language. Ironically, we understand God's anger. Just as a parent has great dreams for a child, so God's great dreams for Jerusalem seem dashed when a sure doom is promised to her.

Parents of teens can understand this passage especially well when they consider that the natural rebelliousness of youth can so easily go too far and become toxic. But instead of resorting to deadly punishments, parents hope and pray for restoration. God is the same kind of parent. God promises in the parable that restoration, even though it is clearly undeserved, will come to Jerusalem. The legitimacy of God's justice cannot be denied, but neither can God's inexorable will that loves us.

Jerusalem at that time was morally bankrupt. God had created this people from a slave nation and made them who they were. God gave them laws so that justice would protect them and provide prosperity. Even after all that, the people took up the religious practices of their neighbors, including infant sacrifice and cult prostitution, and it is in this way that Jerusalem corresponds to the orphan girl turned prostitute in the parable.

Individual responsibility

Chapter 18 of Ezekiel speaks to another aspect of God's justice, the difference between individual responsibility and corporate responsibility. The idea of communal guilt, in which the whole community must take the blame for what individuals do, was taken for granted in Israelite life. You know what that's like. Consider your own school days when a child would run her fingernails along the chalkboard and everyone would shiver. Or think about what happens when a person bites down on a lemon and makes everyone in the room pucker. On the more serious side, consider the communal suffering in war when leaders with their fingers on the nuclear button have the ability to make the whole world pay.

> What does the Lord require of you but to do justice, and to love kindness, and to walk humbly with your God?
>
> Micah 6:8

But now God says that will no longer be the case. Those who are guilty will be punished, but their children will not be held culpable for their actions. Moreover, God offers forgiveness to the guilty, if they will turn away from unfaithfulness, because God does not desire the doom of the sinful! "I have no pleasure in the death of anyone" (18:32).

That can be disappointing to those who want to see sinners pay for their transgressions. Executions in some places are public affairs, supposedly for the edification of children and adults. But people have actually looked forward to executions and considered them a form of entertainment. Often there was great disappointment if the condemned person's sentence was commuted to life in prison. Even today, when executions are held in private, authorities are afraid to commute the sentences of innocent people who have been found guilty, for fear of being labeled soft on crime. People want blood.

Yet if the people say that God is being unfair by forgiving the guilty, God's response is that we're all guilty. And "Yet you say, 'The way of the Lord is not just.' O house of Israel, I will judge all of you according to your ways!" (Ezek. 33:20). As Jesus puts it, "For the measure you give will be the measure you get back"(Luke 6:38b). How much better to allow God's forgiveness, and do as God says: "Turn and live!"

The Watchtower

The final passage reminds us that even though we might be guilty or innocent as individuals, we're still responsible for encouraging—and warning—each other. The parable of the Watchtower sets up a simple transaction. If there's an invader approaching the city and the watchman fails to warn the people and they're destroyed, it's on his head. Conversely, if the watchman sees the invading army approaching and they're destroyed because they ignored his warnings, it's their fault.

We're encouraged to live the parable of the Watchtower. God has sent prophets, like watchmen, to warn us to change our ways. God wants us to turn back, to be forgiven, *to live*!

Things to think about: Talk with others this week about the difference between the legal justice system in your community and God's justice system. Which system would you use to judge others? Why?

> Hope deferred makes the heart sick, but a desire fulfilled is a tree of life.
>
> Proverbs 13:12

Consider this: Sir Arthur Conan Doyle wrote four novels and fifty-six short stories about his famous detective, Sherlock Holmes. According to the writer Robert Keith Leavitt, author of *The Annotated Sherlock Holmes*, "In the 60 cases of record in the Writings, there are 37 definite felonies where the criminal was known to Mr. Sherlock Holmes. In no less than 14 of these did the celebrated detective take the law into his own hands and free the guilty person. In 23 cases the offender was taken by the police. In 7 cases justice was balked by suicide, by death at sea or by other acts of God." I don't know about you, but I prefer justice to the letter of the law, especially when it's my turn to get pulled over on the freeway!

PART II: SESSION

Focus (10 MINUTES)

Take time for announcements and sharing. If you decided to make a relief or survival kit at your last session, present the items you brought at this time. Then choose one of the following activities to focus on the session.

Option A: We often say, "He got his just deserts," meaning that someone got what he deserved. Choose a dessert from a nice tray of goodies that someone prepared ahead of time. Take turns telling what reasons you give yourself for deserving dessert after a meal. Why do you deserve treats?

If treats aren't available, pass around old magazines with pictures of food. Take turns clipping tasty dishes or desserts and pasting them on a piece of newsprint under the label "Just Desserts." Then take turns sharing your rationalizations for dessert.

Option B: Name some of the legal battles raging in our society as you are studying Ezekiel and Daniel. Take turns giving your verdict on the case and suggest an "appropriate" sentence for those involved. What would be fair? What would be right?

Option C: Weigh in on the controversial issue of allowing murder victims' relatives to watch the execution of the murderers. What do proponents hope to gain from such a provision? Why should it or should it not be allowed?

Transition: We're all interested in getting our just deserts when it's something sweet to eat, but who wants to be handed a lemon when they're expecting lemon drops? According to Ezekiel, God wants to give us something sweet, even when we deserve something sour.

Engage the Text (20 MINUTES)
Option A: Quickly share stories of injustice in your life, times when you felt you got the raw end of the deal. Or tell about a time when you got more justice than you asked for, a time when you got better than you deserved. Then listen as someone summarizes the parable of the Orphan, or take turns telling the story, adding details until it is finished. Highlight elements you think are significant from the other passages touched on in this session, such as the image of teeth set on edge and the watchman in the watchtower.

Use the following questions to begin a discussion:
1. How is the parable of the Orphan like your experience of justice or injustice? Do you count on God's grace when you knowingly make a bad decision?
2. Consider the parable of the Orphan. If you had to put yourself in this story, which character would you be? Parent? Orphan? Other?
3. How would the orphan girl tell this story?
4. Look at Ezekiel 18. Which of our actions will harm our children or our children's children? What responsibility do we have for such actions?

5. Who or what has served as a watchman in your life? Are there watchmen in your life now? What warnings should we heed? If it were up to you, what warnings would you give to others?
6. What historical figures or contemporary figures have gotten what they deserved? Who was unjustly punished?

Option B: Participate in a role play. Choose someone in the group to be an intermediary. Then divide into two small groups. One group will represent the orphan. The other group will represent the parent. In small groups, make a list of arguments or write a short letter to the other group, making a case for your side of the argument and pleading for understanding.

When the small groups are done preparing their arguments, hand them to the intermediary who will try to represent the arguments of each group to the other like a judge. Then the intermediary will moderate a discussion between the two groups, making sure that everyone stays in character, speaks in turn, and uses fair arguments. The intermediary will begin the discussion by letting each group respond to the other group's arguments. He or she can then open the discussion for whomever wishes to speak.

In the end, talk about compromise. Who in the biblical story makes concessions? Are there any long-term sacrifices that the orphan makes? How does this story compare to parent/child relationships today?

Respond (15 MINUTES)

Option A: Look at a real life case of justice and injustice and discuss the questions that follow.

Very few nations in the Western Hemisphere practice state execution. The United States is one of them. And in recent years, the number of executions in the United States has risen dramatically. Most of those on death row in the U.S. are male, poor, poorly educated, and many are people of color. In sharp contrast was a woman on death row who was convicted of a very brutal murder. However, she had turned her life around after her death sentence. She converted to Christianity and became a role model to other prisoners and to many Christians.

As her execution date approached, many individuals who usually supported the death penalty spoke on her behalf, claiming that she was a good candidate for commutation. Other proponents of the death penalty demanded that she receive the same justice that she might expect if she were a male or a person of color. Her sentence, despite the attention given to her case, was not commuted and she was executed. Her death caused many people to consider their hard and fast support for the death penalty.

In small groups or as a large group, discuss the following questions:
1. What arguments can you give that support the state's assertion that justice was best served by the execution of the condemned prisoner?
2. What arguments can you give against the execution of a person who has changed for the better?
3. Would you be more likely to be for or against the death penalty if there was a hard and fast option of life in prison without the possibility of parole? Or do you believe that there are circumstances, such as age, health, or repentance, in which a person should be released from prison after a number of years, in spite of their crime?
4. If it were you or a family member in prison, do you think your reaction would be different than if the person were a total stranger?
5. What voice should the victims of crime have in determining the fate of an offender?

Option B: Work together to make a list of undeserved nice things to do for others, such as giving peace offerings, sending cards of support, or sending flowers to someone you're at odds with. Then actually challenge each other to choose someone to give an undeserved gift to in the coming week. If you wish, give your gift anonymously. Make the challenge stronger by choosing partners to check up on each other before the next session. We are more likely to act if we are accountable to a person or group. The next time you meet, talk about the gifts you gave, without naming the person to whom you gave the gift. How did it feel? Was it hard? Was it freeing? How do you think God feels when we receive grace upon grace?

Option C: Talk about where in your own community God's justice is lacking. How can you be agents of God's justice?

Closing (5 MINUTES)
Sing or read together the words of a hymn about God's justice, such as "There's a wideness in God's mercy" or "What does the Lord require." Spend a few minutes in silent meditation, contemplating your own life, the judgment you "deserve," and God's mercy.

Part III: Leader Guidelines

Items Needed
Bibles
Newsprint and markers
Snacks
Magazines with pictures of food
Scissors and glue

Resources
Clements, Ronald E. *Ezekiel* (Westminister Bible Companion series). John Knox Press, 1996.

Tips for Leading
1. Whenever discussing the sins or corruption of others, remind participants that the church is made for sinners, not saints, and that everyone falls short of God's expectations. Discourage blaming and finger-pointing.
2. When participants use derogatory language about others, whether they are people of another faith, race, or ethnicity, try saying, "I'm not comfortable with that term. Let's talk about this person or these people as fellow humans and fellow sinners." Or say, "How are these people different from you and me?"
3. Scan the newspapers and news magazines this week for interesting cases in the court system. Be prepared to use them as examples in the exercises for this session.
4. One of the focus activities calls for desserts. Consider bringing a special treat to the session to highlight the concept of undeserved justice.

Session 3
Apocalypse and Politics

PART I: PREPARATION

Bible passages: Ezekiel 19; 34:20-31; Daniel 9

Key verse: I will save my flock, and they shall no longer be ravaged; and I will judge between sheep and sheep (Ezek. 34:22).

Summary: Ezekiel contrasts the schemings of Hamutal, the shrewd queen of David's dynasty, with the image of a true leader who is a loving shepherd. To this important distinction, Daniel responds, Amen, let us pray! Hamutal is the wife of Josiah and is thought by some to be the lioness in the story who raises up cubs to rule Judah. But Judah learns eventually that it is not really kings and queens who determine things. Even when we think we have control, we're really playing by a different set of rules, God's rules. So if God is in control, what should we the faithful be doing?

Study

Most of us have not been around at the collapse of civilization. The "little" catastrophes we may have experienced in our comfortable world, such as floods and drought, have sometimes paradoxically been the vehicle through which the goodness of human nature is displayed. For instance, in the community where I live, most people of middle age and older remember what is known locally as the Palm Sunday tornado, a vicious storm that struck the area on Palm Sunday in the early 1960s. Some folks' most vivid memories include the kindness of strangers who helped them in their distress.

But elsewhere around the globe we have witnessed the collapse of nations through war, terror, and genocide. In these horrible times, it seems as if ordinary people are forced to make a choice between complying with the madness around them or taking a stand consistent with their

Apocalypse and Politics

faith. To choose faith often means death, but almost certainly vindication later. To choose compliance often means saving one's own life, though collaborators often have much explaining to do later.

Politics and faith

The historical background behind Ezekiel 19 illuminates some of the tensions between playing politics or being God's people. He leaves almost nothing between. To take things into our own hands is certain death. That's why the prophet writes what he does as a dirge or lament. This is a dirge for the nation Israel, who has been proud and disobedient to the covenant with God. But it is also a lament for specific individuals. King Josiah, who attempted to draw the people back into a right relationship with God, died after a thirty-one-year reign, in a battle with the Egyptians in the year 609 B.C. He was succeeded by his son Jehoahaz, who ruled a bare three months. In Ezekiel's lament, he suggests that this lion cub met an early death because he was cruel (19:3-4).

> We are not going away.
> We are not going away.
> God blesses the people who stand up and say
> We are not going away.
>
> —Lee Krahenbuhl

Another of Josiah's sons, Jehoiakim, took the throne, and ruled eleven years, but he was a vassal of Nebechadnezzar of Babylon, who actually controlled the country. His son, Jehoiachin (notice the slight difference in spelling), followed him, but ruled only three months. Both father and son are remembered in the Bible as evil kings.

The next king, Zedekiah, ruled eleven years, from 597–586 B.C. He was Jehoahaz's brother, and the two shared the same mother, Hamutal, in contrast to their brother Jehoiakim. Under Zedekiah's watch the nation was finally destroyed by the Babylonians, and many of the people were led into captivity.

All of these kings, no matter who their mothers were, treated their own people with cruelty and seemed preoccupied with expanding or preserving their own political power, at the expense of the people. While commentators agree that the lioness mentioned in Ezekiel 19 is probably Israel, some suggest she also stands for Hamutal, who would have been working in the background to see that her sons occupied the throne. In the face of a national disaster and the dissolution of their country, those who were responsible for the people did not seek to lead them back to the true worship of God, but instead fought to cement their personal place of power in a crumbling kingdom.

In contrast, the passage from Ezekiel 34 relies on the classic picture of the king as shepherd and suggests that it will take the Divine Shepherd to straighten things out. The false shepherds described in the first nineteen verses of the chapter have failed to tend to God's people, those who are outcasts, those who are sick, injured, and have strayed.

A false shepherd, like a self-serving, power-hungry king, sees his charges as a commodity, a product that is to be exploited for personal benefit. The true shepherd loves the sheep and seeks rich pasture for their welfare. "I will seek the lost, and I will bring back the strayed, and I will bind up the injured, and I will strengthen the weak, but the fat and the strong I will destroy. I will feed them with justice," the shepherd says in Ezekiel 34:16.

> Our Father, who art in heaven,
> Hallowed be thy name.
> Thy kingdom come,
> Thy will be done,
> On earth as it is in heaven.
> Give us this day our daily bread,
> And forgive us our debts
> As we forgive our debtors.
> And lead us not into temptation
> But deliver us from evil
> For thine is the kingdom, the power, and the glory, forever.
> Amen.

Prayer works
The prayer and vision in Daniel 9 is set in yet another time of political transition for Israel. The Babylonian threat was passed. Judah's rulers chose the quest for power over piety and landed themselves squarely in that mess. But now even their captors have been conquered, and Daniel comes before God in the first year of the reign of Babylon's conqueror. In his prayer of confession, Daniel calls to mind Jeremiah's prophecy that the Babylonians would reign over them only seventy years, which was fairly accurate. Instead of pleading for God's help to escape oppression, he comes before God in an attitude of prayer and confession. Daniel confesses his own sins, the sins of his people, and makes it clear that he does not come before God as one who has a right to expect God's deliverance. His confession is an admission of how much the people rely on God.

Daniel's prayer is preceded by fasting. It is important to note that in the biblical tradition a fast is not used to despair of the evil world. Scripture has a high view of creation. God declared that all these things were good. Rather, fasting focuses the mind and the heart. And in later biblical tradition, fasting is the prelude to battle. For Daniel, of course, all battle is spiritual and not physical. His own faith is a testimony to the fact that nonviolent resistance is an effective means of resisting tyrants. The real quarrel is not between us and the tyrants, but between God and the

Apocalypse and Politics

tyrants, and the visions and stories of Daniel make it clear who will be the victor.

As he prays Daniel recalls God's saving history, bringing to mind the exodus, even though it means remembering Israel's disobedience in the desert as well. By bringing up both kinds of events, Daniel points to the success of God's efforts and the ultimate failure of our own. This leads to a final confession and a plea for God's forgiveness and action.

A visit from Gabriel
The Divine response is quick: "…while I was speaking in prayer, the man Gabriel, whom I had seen before in a vision, came to me in swift flight…" (9:21). However, Gabriel's reply seems about as obvious as VCR instructions. When it's all sorted out, Gabriel is suggesting a new interpretation of the seventy years of Israelite captivity prophesied by Jeremiah. Seventy weeks or years (every seven years is a week), or seven times seventy, comes to 490 years or the period of time before the temple in Jerusalem will be restored after the exile. If a week equals seven years, Gabriel reveals in 9:27 that in the middle of the second century before Christ the evil ruler Antiochus will interrupt worship in the temple for three and a half years.

> We wish to inform you that tomorrow we will be killed with our families.
>
> —Letter from a Ruwandan to a pastor

On the one hand the 490 years doesn't work out quite right. The period of time from Daniel's prayer to the death of Antiochus is about 430 years. Push it back to Jeremiah's reckoning and it comes to 441 years. On the other hand, the three and a half years of trouble that Antiochus gives Israel works out just about right.

But the arithmetical accuracy of either statement is immaterial. It's not the quantity but the quality of the numbers that matter in the Bible. Seven is a number that implies completeness or wholeness. Seventy years in this instance expresses the idea that a period of penance has drawn to a close. By contrast, three and a half years signifies that something has been cut short, ended early. It is appropriate that God's people see that when the time is complete, God's power will be displayed, and God's sovereignty over history will be made apparent. Conversely, earthly tyrants who usurp God's place should know that despite their best plans their time will be cut short.

According to Daniel, there is always a present persecution that is drawing to a close in every age. We have to hang on. Our decision whether to conform to the expectations of the world, taking things into our own hands, or whether to conform to our faith should be based on that knowledge. Even when we win, we can only bask in our victory a short time before the next horror appears.

One response, which is always appropriate in these circumstances, is to pray. That is what Daniel does. His language is not predictive but descriptive. Numerologists will gain no benefit from Daniel—or Revelation—if they come at it with a calculator. These are numbers that speak to the heart and not the head. Or as John Goldingay, who wrote a commentary on Daniel, puts it so well: "The period of deepest oppression did last about three and a half years, but that is not the point. This is not prognostication or prediction. It is promise."

Things to think about: Pray for others this week. Avoid praying that things will work out well for them. Rather pray that the people in your prayers will have the strength to endure the particular stress they are under.

Also, reflect on your own endurance under stress. Have you ever felt the strength of others praying for you? When? How did it feel? To hear someone pray for us in times of trouble, as in an anointing service, can be a special balm. "I'll remember you in prayer" can be the most important words ever spoken by a Christian.

Part II: Session

Focus (5 minutes)

Take time for announcements and sharing. If you chose to send undeserved messages or gifts after the last session, report on your actions. How did they go? Was your act anonymous? How did the receiver respond?

Choose one of the following activities to focus on the session.

Option A: Play a game of checkers with the person next to you. This is a special game of strategy. Attached to the game pieces are self-sticking notes with the names of children and adults in the congregation or relatives (such as mother, father, sister, or brother, husband, wife, son, daugh-

Apocalypse and Politics

ter). Play the game quickly, in five minutes or less. Try to win by sacrificing as few of your loved ones as possible.

Transition: Sometimes the strategy of a game requires that we sacrifice a game piece for ultimate victory. When we sacrificed pieces with the names of special people on them, we may not have been touched deeply, but there are powerful people who move others around the political chessboard everyday and are willing to sacrifice them as readily as pawns. It happened in Ezekiel and Daniel's day, too. Look at the text for this session to see how we should respond.

Option B: Make fast decisions. In three minutes, answer the following questions. The answers are at the end of the session in Tips for Leaders. If you prefer, break into pairs and quiz each other.
1. Recite Psalm 23.
2. How many wise men came to visit Jesus after his birth?
3. What was Peter doing when the Lord lowered a sheet containing unclean animals?
4. Name one of Job's three friends?
5. Name one of the two spies who returned a good report to Moses?
6. Recite the Lord's Prayer.
7. How many brothers did Jesus have, according to the Gospels?
8. What sort of creature swallowed up Jonah?
9. According to the Bible, who lived the longest life, and how old was he when he died?

Transition: At the end of three minutes, look at the answers to the quiz together. Don't bother comparing your results. The point is (although we wish we had a lot of time for the tough choices) that sometimes we have to think fast on our feet. Ezekiel and Daniel lived in times that called for fast thinking. They urge us to respond quickly in obedience to our faith instead of responding for ourselves.

Engage the Text (20 MINUTES)
Option A: As a group, scour Ezekiel 19 for words or images that describe a leader as the world defines a leader. Make a list on newsprint. Then examine Ezekiel 34:20-31 for images of leadership as God defines it. Also list these traits on newsprint. Then discuss the following questions:
1. Are all worldly leaders evil? Give examples of good and bad leaders whom you know of from history or current events.

2. Are godly leaders always successful? Give examples of godly leaders who were successful and those who were not.
3. What do you think "success" is, according to Ezekiel or Daniel?
4. How important is success to the prophets?
5. In your view, what is important to the prophets?
6. Do the prophets promise that life will be fine if the people are faithful?
7. How will we know when we've held on long enough?

Option B: Daniel's response to crisis is to pray a prayer of confession and repentance. Look at two other prayers in the Bible for comparison. How do Psalm 23 (a prayer in the face of danger or death) and the Lord's Prayer (Matt. 6:9-13) compare to Daniel's prayer? Look for these characteristics in each:
1. Adoration
2. Confession
3. Covenant
4. Petition (request for aid)

Talk together about how you think prayer works. In what sense does prayer work on God? In what sense does prayer work on you?

Option C: Review the headlines in the morning paper. Where are the political hot spots in the world today? What critical decisions do politicians and leaders have to make? How would you respond as a leader in difficult times? How do you think you would respond as an ordinary citizen in difficult times?

Respond (20 MINUTES)
Option A: Have a discussion about prayer using the following discussion starters.
1. Daniel prays by himself but he uses the word "we." What are the "we" prayers you need to pray this week.
2. Do you prefer to pray your own words or those of another? Whose? What style of prayer works best for you?
3. When has someone prayed for you? What were they praying about? What did God's answer seem to be?
4. What time, if any, do you intentionally set aside for prayer?
5. Can you think of prayers uttered in times of distress that were answered? How long did it take for an answer to come?
6. Do prayers always have answers?
7. Are prayers of confession part of your regular prayer life? Discuss the importance of confession in your life.

8. What is the place of prayer in crisis? Does it do any good? Is it your first resort or your last resort?
9. As a group write a prayer for the people, however you define "the people." Covenant to pray that prayer at a specific time for a specific period of time wherever each of you might happen to be.

Option B: Consider a covenant of prayer for the upcoming week. Agree on a time in which all members of the group will pray, at whatever place you find yourselves. Agree on a focus for prayer. You might pray for the larger ministry of the church, a specific person, or a particular issue that is besetting society or church at this time.

As an alternative, write your name on a slip of paper and put it with the names of others in the group in an envelope. Or substitute names of world leaders, denominational leaders, or community leaders in place of your own name. Draw out a name, making sure you don't get your own name, and commit yourself to praying for the person whose name you drew. Pray daily for the individual. Model your prayer after Daniel's prayer of petition and endurance.

Closing (5 MINUTES)
Say the Lord's Prayer in unison. The text appears as a sidebar in this session for those who don't know it by heart.

PART III: LEADER GUIDELINES

Items Needed
Bibles
Several sets of checkers, with names attached to the pieces
Newsprint and markers
Paper and an envelope
Current newspaper or news magazine

Tips for Leading
1. Set aside time during the week to prepare for the session. Avoid waiting until an hour before the session to prepare. Try this schedule:
Day 1: Reflect on the previous lesson; then read the lesson for this week, taking time to read all the biblical texts involved.
Day 2: Read the focus activity and picture how you will lead that portion of the lesson.

Day 3: Don't even think about the upcoming session. Let it percolate into your life.

Day 4: Focus on the Study portion of the upcoming session. What questions come to mind that the group may want to discuss? How can you ask questions in an open-ended way, so that participants must answer with more than a yes or no.

Day 5: Read through the lesson again, focusing on the Respond and Closing sections. This would be a good day to call and remind those who may have agreed to take a specific responsibility for the upcoming session.

Day 6: Set aside ten minutes for prayer about the lesson.

Day 7: Relax. The session is in God's hands.

2. Use these answers for the Bible quiz in Focus, Option B.
   1) See Psalm 23.
   2) Two or more. Scripture doesn't give the number.
   3) He was sleeping and having a vision.
   4) Bildad, Eliphaz, and Zophar.
   5) Joshua and Caleb.
   6) See Matthew 6:9-13.
   7) Four
   8) A great fish.
   9) Methuselah. He lived for 969 years.
3. Encourage people who are reticent to speak by offering them the first opportunity to contribute to discussion. Ask those who speak often to wait until others have shared.
4. Prayer can be a very private matter, especially prayers of confession. Do not put people on the spot by asking them to confess their shortcomings.
5. Invite participants to bring a school yearbook for the next meeting.

Session 4
Sins and Sensibility

Part I: Preparation

Bible passages: Ezekiel 4–5; 8; 25; Daniel 7

Key verse: He said to me, "Mortal, do you see what they are doing, the great abominations that the house of Israel are committing here, to drive me far from my sanctuary? Yet you will see still greater abominations" (Ezek. 8:6).

Summary: Prophetic words about sin are hard to accept and even harder to heed. In these chapters from Ezekiel, God gives the prophet some eye-catching, head-turning techniques for getting the prophetic word out, such as visual models, street theater, exaggeration, and even ordinary down-home images like hair. If that's not enough to convince the people to change, there is always the threat of Babylonian exile or defeat at the hands of the tyrant Antiochus Epiphanes. In the face of all these warnings, however, God's people keep on sinning. We know how that is. We, like they, feel that sin is someone else's fault, or sin is inevitable so why try to avoid it. After all, God gave us free will. What does God expect? Then again, God also makes choices. What should we expect from the God we've sinned against?

Study

Legos building blocks. A bad hair day. And a hole-in-the-wall place. What do these things have in common? They're all devices Ezekiel used to get his listeners' attention. In the story, he's speaking to God's people who were taken away to Babylon in the first wave of exiles. A greater, more terrible fate would come in the second wave to those in Jerusalem who were waiting it out, playing a dangerous political game for survival.

Ezekiel's message, I think, is to show people how ugly their sins are and what sort of consequences will be the result. Sin can be prettified and justified, redefined so it is no longer sin in the eyes of some. This is the kind of logic that led some Israelites to feel that it was not their unfaithfulness, but God's inability to protect them from enemies, that drove them to worship the gods of other nations. They had neatly absolved themselves of the problem and blamed God. Ezekiel knows he has to at least try to get the attention of these people, no matter what it takes, before it is too late. If that takes a series of odd actions that might lead some people to think he is crazy, so be it. The message is that important.

Unfortunately, the prophet's message up to this point (wake up and stop sinning before things get worse) has become stale, and the people are no longer paying attention. Maybe they have a short attention span. Or maybe the prophet has droned on too long. Perhaps they think the worst has already happened and their fate will improve soon. Whatever their reasoning, they have not stopped sinning, nor have they bothered to consider the effects of sin.

> Midway in our life's journey,
> I went astray
> From the straight road and
> woke to find myself
> alone in a dark wood.
>
> —Dante, *The Divine Comedy*, Inferno
> I, 1-3 (John Ciardi translation)

The situation escalates

Dramatic times called for dramatic prophecy. That is what Ezekiel does—drama. His first bit of street theater involves a game played with toys essentially. He takes a brick and draws a picture of Jerusalem upon it. He then builds a siegeworks, and a wall, and ramps, and camps, and battering rams. These things are meant to be signs of the coming siege of Jerusalem.

Ezekiel's second act of street theater is a public display of his infirmity. He lies for long periods of time first on one side of his body and then on the other. This sign points to the length of the punishment that will be meted out to God's people for their long years of apostasy. For the third sign, Ezekiel gives a cooking demonstration for a starvation diet, signifying the short rations that will accompany the siege.

Then, for the fourth sign, it's show time. Step right up and see the famed prophet cut off his hair! A third of his hair is chopped and diced, a third is cast to the wind, and a third is burnt. Only a few hairs, signifying the remnant, the faithful survivors, are saved.

It would be hard to watch some of these exhibitions without asking at some point what all this means. And that would give Ezekiel the chance to explain God's message. If he had simply stood on the street corner and

Sins and Sensibility

handed out tracts, people would have thrown them in the first trash can they saw, accusing him of being overly pious and pushy.

What is Ezekiel up to? Someone has to tell the people that things are not right. Someone has to cause God's people to take a good look at the ugly consequences of sin in order to even consider the possibility of change. There is a bit of good news, too. One essential element of the prophetic warning is an out—if people change. The "day of the Lord" scriptures in the Old Testament provide a gloomy picture of the future, but they always contain the possibility that the future can be averted if the people change.

> I am the way into the city of woe.
> I am the way to a forsaken people.
> I am the way to eternal sorrow.
> Sacred justice moved my architect.
> I was raised here by divine omnipotence,
> Primordial love and ultimate intellect.
> Only those elements time cannot wear
> Were made before me, and beyond time I stand.
> Abandon all hope ye who enter here.
>
> — Dante, *The Divine Comedy*, Inferno III, 1-9

Looking into the future

Alas, many times people do not change, even when the warning is abundantly clear. In the eighth chapter of Ezekiel, in what appears to be a vision, Ezekiel is transported by a heavenly being to distant Jerusalem, to the temple. This humanlike being takes him to a hole in the wall and tells him to widen it and take a look inside.

To his horror, various abominations are taking place. Whether these acts were actually taking place in the temple is not the point. If these were the practices of the people in their daily lives, then this is what their worship amounted to, because whatever we do in our daily routine is our true witness to the faith.

First recognizing that something is wrong is essential to change. Ask almost anyone with a chronic medical problem, such as heart disease, diabetes, or high blood pressure, and they can probably tell you that there were signs of the disease that they ignored early on. If they had paid attention, they could have gotten an early diagnosis and valuable treatment. The treatment of a disease, though, often includes a radical change of lifestyle. Individuals usually make these changes in the short term, but in the long term many will return to the lifestyle that contributed to their difficulties.

Daniel's vision

Ezekiel and the humanlike figure try to make an early diagnosis, pointing ahead to a terrible judgment that is coming against God's people, as well as other nations (see Ezek. 25). Daniel also witnesses a terrible judgment in the future. And he also sees a humanlike figure in the vision. But in his account (Dan. 7), the one "like a human being" will pronounce judgment on the people, descending from heaven in glory and power. This terrible figure is the Son of Man, who looks a lot like Jesus. And therein lies our hope.

Among the elements in Daniel's dreams is the use of animals to represent other nations. Paul Lederach, author of *Daniel* (Believers Church Bible Commentary), points out that in our own time owls still represent wisdom, chickens cowardice, and eagles strength. Each of the beasts in this vision is an unclean animal according to Jewish law. They represent the Gentiles at their worst. The first, the lion with majestic wings, is lordlike and swift to kill in judgment. It represents the Babylonians. The code of Hammurabi, an ancient set of laws that lifted whole societies out of a moral chaos, were still heavily weighted toward the strong and away from the weak. Contrast God's law revealed on Mt. Sinai, the Ten Commandments, which are meant to be applied to the rich as well as poor, weak as well as strong, king as well as subject. King David, for instance, thought he was exempt from the Commandments when he looked on Bathsheba in lust, but he was wrong.

The second beast is the bear, representing the Medes. It is told to "Arise, devour many bodies!" (7:5). Empires lie broken at its feet. But it is not the last of the beasts, for a leopard-like being also arises. This winged creature represents the Persians. Swiftly like the leopard, they created their empire on the foundations of conquered cultures, such as Ur, Ebla, Sumer, and the "eternal" city of Babylon.

> They have committed false report; moreover, they have spoken untruths; secondarily, they are slanders; sixth and lastly, they have belied a lady; thirdly, they have verified unjust things, and to conclude, they are lying knaves.
>
> —William Shakespeare, Much Ado About Nothing, IV, i, 34

Timing is everything

As the account goes, Daniel is having this vision during the first year of Babylon's last king, the ill-fated Belshazzar, but the events are a veiled way of speaking about the trials of God's people during the Maccabean crisis in the second century before Jesus. At that time Israel was struggling under the seemingly eternal grip of Antiochus IV Epiphanes. He is represented by the fourth beast who is terrible and dreadful and exceedingly strong, with great iron teeth, ten horns, and tramping feet. The monster, at first representing the glorious empire of Alexander the Great, begins to sprout a new little horn that supplants three others, pulling them up by the roots, and suddenly the beast becomes a successor of Alexander, Antiochus IV. Interestingly, the horn has human features, especially arrogance.

This monster represented the present crisis for many of the people who were reading Daniel's prophecies. They lived under the thumb of Antiochus, who desecrated the temple, halted sacrifices, tortured children, and scattered the nation. So Judah looked to the stories of its ancestors living under earlier persecution to understand why.

But who will stand against the beast when God's people are weak and scattered like sheep? None other than the perfect shepherd who is a sheep like they and who will sacrifice himself for them. Daniel's vision is that such a shepherd is coming who is far more powerful than any worldly king. He is the lamb, who in Revelation appears with the mark of sacrifice but who is the champion over the beast.

But in this vision we see the lamb as he really is, the Ancient of Days. His throne is fiery flames and there are wheels of burning fires. He is attended by uncounted heavenly beings. Maybe the beasts aren't so powerful after all. Even though the fourth beast is filling the air with "the noise of its arrogant words" (7:11), it is destroyed effortlessly.

You wanted a terrible God? You've got one. The pure images even of heaven seem too terrifying to endure. But this God is filtered for his followers through "one like a human being, coming with the clouds of heaven" (7:13). To this one is given power and dominion. Many Christians identify this one, who is like a human being (in other translations called "son of man"), to be Jesus. The New Testament uses language in its own apocalyptic sections that also identify Jesus with this person of power. So now the prophecy is for the exiles in Babylon, the persecuted under Antiochus, and for Christians, the sheep of God's pasture.

We're going to win.
We're going to win. That's the central message of the scripture. No matter how horrible the monster, we're going to win. Each day there are new headlines. Old monsters are relegated to the back pages and a new enemy emerges. But in the vision of Daniel, kingdoms that should last forever fade away in the face of our God. First-century Christians daringly proclaimed that the Jesus, so brutally executed, defeated death and in fact arose from the dead and would return in glory. And, though, for these early Christians

Antiochus was a dead memory, it is now Nero who is the brutal reality. The words of Daniel provide comfort, encouragement, and reassurance.

The struggle goes on. The Anabaptists who were brutally persecuted by state churches would have been right in associating the beasts in Daniel with those who mocked Christ by killing in his name. And we are correct in drawing parallels between the beast and people and events in our own time. So will our children and our children's children.

Swiftly they rise and swiftly they fall, at least in retrospect. We are meant to take comfort from empires that pass away with the wind. What would be nonsense to their persecutors is abundantly clear to God's people living under persecution in any age and reading Daniel's dream. It makes visible to the faithful what is invisible to the unfaithful—the saving action of God through history.

In our time we have been confronted by dreams and visions of different sorts. Take Dr. Martin Luther King, Jr., for instance. He had a dream, and his dream still inspires us. The sinners who opposed him and the Civil Rights movement have been repudiated, or they have repented, as was the case with Governor George Wallace. While in the moment, God's action seemed remote, even undetectable, the action of God's spirit was more powerful than racism and hatred. Its action uproots more lives than any tornado.

Things to think about: Read parts of Dante's *The Divine Comedy*. This fourteenth-century poem draws together everything that was known of religion, science, geography, history, literature, and politics into one great epic, which revolves on that most essential act, the salvation of a single soul. After reading some of his images of hell, consider your own definition of hell or unbearable suffering. Why do you think God allows this kind of suffering in the world?

Part II: Session

Focus (5 minutes)
Greet each other and share announcements. Then choose one of these options to focus on the topic of the session.

Option A: Share your school yearbook with the group and look at the yearbooks others brought. Look especially for interesting or unmanaged hair! What do hairstyles say about the people who wear them?

Transition: Ezekiel knew all about bad hair days. At one time God directed him to cut off his hair in a symbolic action that attracted a lot of attention to what he was doing.

Option B: Share a meaningful dream you've had recently. What did you learn from your dream? What did your dream tell you to do? To what extent did your dream rise out of feelings of guilt or inadequacy?

Transition: Truths or insights often come to us in our dreams. Daniel used inspired dreams to reveal God's truth to people who desperately needed to hear God's word.

Option C: Lay out magazines and encourage members to cut out pictures that are dreamlike, perhaps even illustrating a particular dream in an apocalyptic fashion. Work together to quickly make a single collage, posting it for the entire group to see during the session.

Transition: Many times, truths or insights come to us in our dreams. Daniel used inspired dreams to reveal God's truth to people who desperately needed to hear God's word.

Engage the Text (30 MINUTES)

Option A: Divide into three groups to focus on one of the theatrical actions of Ezekiel in Ezekiel 4–5 (building a model of siegeworks, lying on his side, or cutting his hair). Each group will choose one of the three dramas, outlining the action on a sheet of newsprint exactly what Ezekiel did. Then, in your small groups, consider the following questions. Choose a reporter who will share a summary of your discussion with the larger group.

1. What do you think Ezekiel was attempting to show through his actions? How effective do you think he was? How effective would he be if he were performing the same actions today?
2. What would you do to get someone's attention with a vitally important message? How dramatic would you need to be to get a stranger's attention? a loved one's attention?
3. As a small group decide what you would like to say to your community about sin. Think of a dramatic action that could be done in a public place that would grab everyone's attention. Who in your group has the most credibility to enact such a drama in the community? Why?

Return to the large group to report on your small group discussion.

Session 4

Option B: Ezekiel's bad hair day and his other attention-getting activities were designed to help his people see the ugly reality behind their pretty sins. Look back over the texts for this session. What sins are the people committing? How have they masked their sins? What is the result?

Divide into small groups or remain together in a large group. Work on a definition of sin. Post your work on newsprint or a chalkboard. Then use the following questions for discussion about sin:
1. What does it take to get people to take unpleasant news seriously, such as a medical diagnosis or rejection?
2. What does it take to get people to realize their sin?
3. Does Ezekiel say that God will always bail us out of our sin?
4. Do Ezekiel and Daniel believe that humans can overcome sinning? If so, how?
5. Other than our own weaknesses, what factors contribute to our sinning, such as the political systems we inherit, our family history, or "society"? What is our responsibility for sin, and how much belongs to others? Whose responsibility is it to change things?

Option C: The Bible points not only to sin, but also to solutions. One of those solutions, which appeared both in damning scriptures and saving scriptures, is the vision of the Son of Man in Daniel's dream. The dream points to specific empires and enemies, but as the commentary points out, these could be authentically reinterpreted as dangers in our own time without damaging the text, as long as we don't insist we have the exclusive and sole authentic interpretation. Discuss the following questions:
1. Part of the message of both Ezekiel and Daniel is that in the face of these dramatic messages, change is possible for individuals and nations. Do you feel in control of your life?
2. Can you make changes easily? Do you have a lot of will power or none? How much outside intervention, either through human or divine help, have you needed to make serious changes?
3. Was it too late for Judah and Israel to change? Why or why not? When is it too late to change in your own life?

Respond (10 MINUTES)

Option A: Look together at the portion of the study included in this session that talks about the exotic nature of Ezekiel's attention-getting devices. Then leaf through magazines or newspapers, pointing out the most effective advertising devices for consumers. How would you translate these into advertisements against sin and for faithfulness? What gets the attention of church people? Is guilt persuasive? the threat of eternal damnation? Why or why not?

Option B: The group leader might turn the group's attention to Daniel's dream. Share some of the information in the study. Dreams, like advertising schemes, can get our attention. Consider some of the following questions.
1. Call to mind an especially vivid or prophetic dream. Are there elements you would be willing to share with the group? Was the vivid dream as powerful to others when you told them about it as when you experienced it?
2. When has the church or other people of faith encouraged you to "dream dreams" and "see visions"? Whom have you encouraged to do the same?
3. Share vivid experiences or dreams that seemed shattering at the time. Do these have the same impact when repeated out loud as they did upon waking? Try to visualize the dreams of others.
4. Is there a passage of a book or a poem that has affected you deeply, but which seems to make no impact on others when you share it? If our young people have visions and our older members dream dreams, do we allow them to be shared, or do we discount their ideas?
5. Dream dreams and see visions together. What impossibles would you like to see the group, your congregation, or yourself accomplish for the work of Christ?
6. How do we know that we can trust dreams and visions? How do we test them?

Option C: As one group, or in small groups, brainstorm possible activities to attract attention to the church, God, or your congregation. Stretch your minds. Write down all ideas, no matter how outrageous they seem. Then evaluate the list. Are any of these ideas possible? Choose and plan one activity to actually carry out as a group for the church or the community.

Closing (2 MINUTES)
Pray together the prayer of St. Francis.

Lord,
make me an instrument of your peace.
Where there is hatred, let me sow love;
   where there is injury, pardon;
   where there is doubt, faith;
   where there is despair, hope;

> where there is darkness, light;
> where there is sadness, joy.
> O divine Master,
> > grant that I may not so much seek
> > > to be consoled, as to console;
> > > to be understood, as to understand;
> > > to be loved, as to love.
> > For it is in giving, that we receive;
> > > it is in pardoning that we are pardoned;
> > > it is in dying that we are born to eternal life. Amen.

PART III: LEADER GUIDELINES

Items Needed
Bibles
Chalkboard or newsprint and markers
School yearbooks
Old magazines

Tips for Leading
1. When asking participants to share personal stories of dreams or sins, for instance, let them volunteer responses. Do not single out people for responses or insist that everyone respond. Personal stories may be too painful to share.
2. The passages in this unit are long. Be sure to read them all and be prepared to summarize them for regular participants, as well as visitors who might not be familiar with the text.
3. On the other hand, strongly encourage each participant to read the study before coming to the session. Preparation will make discussion more fruitful.
4. Consult a one-volume commentary on these passages, or read the introduction and study notes on the passage in a study Bible. Look in an encyclopedia for information on Alexander the Great and Antiochus IV Epiphanes. Get an idea of world history in the second and third centuries before Christ.
5. Look for a copy of "The Last Flower" by James Thurber, for the class to read together. A copy is probably in one of Thurber's several collections.

Session 5
The Visions Have Not Ceased

Part I: Preparation

Bible passages: Ezekiel 12:17-25; 20:1-44; Daniel 6:19-28

Key verse: Mortal, what is this proverb of yours about the land of Israel, which says, "The days are prolonged, and every vision comes to nothing"? Tell them therefore, "Thus says the Lord God: I will put an end to this proverb..." (Ezek.12:22-23).

Summary: At the same time the apocalyptic writers are urging the people to hold on as long as it takes, they are assuring God's people that their suffering won't be forever. In these chapters, Ezekiel responds to the discouraged who say there are no more visions. He says, in fact, that visions are always coming true. For proof he recounts in chapter 20 the history of God's people in the desert and God's saving acts despite their many transgressions. Then, after likening the desert experience to the present, Ezekiel affirms that God is going to save the people again in spite of their stubbornness. Will we operate by the same pattern of failure and rescue in the future, or can we learn from our past and make a change in the future?

Study

There are Bible times and then there are our times. Bible times are about shepherds on hillsides and stiff-necked people and saints with halos. Our times include cell phones, laptop computers, and fashions that change at the speed of light. Not much connection there. Right?

Wrong. To the naysayer prophets of doom who complain that "The days are prolonged, and every vision comes to nothing," Ezekiel says, "Bunk." God's response to that gloomy outlook, through the prophet, is that visions are coming, golden bright from heaven's gate, and that these visions are being fulfilled right now. God is not presenting some vague moral code for a perfect time somewhere in the distant future. God's words are for right now.

Then to show how current this message really is, Ezekiel is told to recount the history of God's people in the desert. Oppressed and enslaved, God called the people out of slavery, but they insisted on returning to abominable gods who did nothing for them. So God gave them the Ten Commandments, a few boundaries meant to enhance life. And God also made them witnesses to wonders beyond anyone's imagination, yet in Ezekiel's account, they sin again and again, earning God's wrath, yet never receiving the full measure. God determined on more than one occasion to scatter the people Israel to the four winds, but spared them, as much for the sake of the name of Yahweh as for theirs.

> Been there. Done that.
> —t-shirt slogan

Even after they reached the Promised Land and saw the fulfillment of the dream given centuries before to Abraham, Isaac, and Jacob, they continued to worship the horrid gods of their neighbors. They are still sinning, Ezekiel suggests, as they had in the desert, but God will respond by bringing them to the holy mountain to, of all things, create a nation apart that will be a light to all the nations.

This last part of the message is directed to Israelites in Babylon, the victims of the first wave of deportation. Ezekiel encourages them to see themselves as part of the fulfillment of scripture, of God's wrath justly directed against a straying people who have sullied his name among the nations of the world. They are to call to mind the straying of Israel in the desert and take it personally. But they are also to remind themselves that ultimately this nation of sinners was justified by God and taken to the Promised Land. So too, these exiles will come to the Promised Land again. The present generation may die off, as did the rebellious generation hundreds of years before, but God's promise is fulfilled generation after generation. There is renewal. There is resurrection. There is hope! This is, after all, a living God, and this God saves. This God delivers! This God never forgets the people!

Daniel

The first five chapters of Daniel recount the prophet's adventures and God's mighty acts during the Babylonian captivity. Daniel survived everything that the enemies of God threw at him. And finally, with the fall of Babylon, God's people find themselves ruled by the Persians who will relieve their suffering. After all the stories of warning and judgment, it's time for the case to be made again that God's people have a God who delivers and saves.

By the beginning of this story, Daniel would have been an old man. Whether he was taken to Babylon in 604 or 597 B.C. with one of the two waves of captives, this story, set after the year 539 B.C., indicates Daniel was probably in his late seventies or his eighties. Age proved to be no barrier to his faithfulness.

In Daniel 10:6, we learn that Daniel could be clearly seen through the windows as he prayed, which raises an interesting point. Jesus counseled his disciples to pray in secret so only the Father in heaven would know. Was Daniel acting contrary to this? Perhaps. But Jesus was speaking to those who hoped to gain a better public reputation because of their public piety. Daniel wasn't praying in public to improve his reputation. In fact, he was putting his very life in danger by doing it. Bible commentator John Goldingay makes an interesting point: "When prayer is fashionable it is time to pray in secret (Matt 6:5-6), but when prayer is under pressure, to pray in secret is to give the appearance of fearing the king more than God."

Those who fail to learn from the past are condemned to repeat it.

Early Christians faced the same choice—obey God or earthly rulers. In some cases Christians were delivered from destruction, as in Peter's case when he was released from prison. But in other circumstances, Christians were executed for their faith, such as Stephen and James, the brother of the Lord. But their deaths were their victories, for their martyrdom proved the ultimate validation of their faith.

Daniel's story was one of deliverance rather than martyrdom not only for him, but for a non-Jew as well—King Darius. Because fire was sacred in the Zoroastrian faith of the Persians, it was not used as a means of capital punishment. Instead, Daniel was thrown to the lions. Note that like Pilate, King Darius feels trapped by the law he allowed himself to be talked into.

The fact is that on certain occasions the law is unjust and must be disobeyed. The practice of breaking the law for the sake of righteousness is called civil disobedience. Based on justice and truth, civil disobedience is one of the few strengths the persecuted have. They draw courage from their weakness through the righteousness of their cause. Those who are weak can still triumph, because God favors them. Their cause is a holy cause.

Daniel used civil disobedience. By remaining faithful in the face of persecution, Daniel became a light to the nations. According to author Daniel Smith-Christopher, Mahatma Gandhi said he "found much consolation in reading the book of the prophet Daniel in the Bible." Gandhi stated that Daniel was "one of the greatest passive resisters that ever lived" and took great solace in the book during his work in South Africa and India.

> What's past is prologue.
> —Shakespeare, The Tempest, II, I, 57

The powers respond to nonviolence with violence, hate, and deception, because they know it is dangerous and powerful and a threat to their authority. Sometimes they try to portray the nonviolent as violent to turn public opinion against the holy cause. But in this case, the king is persuaded by Daniel's witness. King Darius is horrified that he must condemn a trusted counselor to death for the crime of praying three times a day. He consigns Daniel to his fate anyway but expresses the hope that Daniel's God will deliver him. After a sleepless night, Darius unseals the pit and discovers Daniel is alive. Until this point Daniel has said nothing; when he speaks it is to proclaim God's glory and great deeds.

Perhaps the most important thing about the story is that Darius, a pagan king, proclaims Daniel's God as "…the living God" (6:26). It's not just God's people who proclaim this. Nonbelievers and nonbelieving nations come to believe, too. In contrast to gods of stone and gold, the message of the nations from this portion of Daniel is that God is active in history. God is not remote but living, listening to the people and delivering them at will. Though empires fall and rise, God does not cease to speak or act and to this day remains true.

Things to think about: Poll your friends, family, and co-workers this week. Find out if they are hopeful about the future, what visions they have, and how near God seems to them. Also find out from the same people whether we can truly learn from our mistakes. Ask them to give concrete examples. Bring stories with you to the session.

Part II: Session

Focus (10 minutes)
Take time for sharing and announcements. Then choose one of the options below to focus on the topic of the session.

Option A: Play the game Conjunction. In the game each player makes a three-part statement. In the first part, justify yourself. In the second part, be mildly disparaging of a companion. In the third part, be critical of someone else. It demonstrates the way we treat ourselves, present company, and those who are absent. Here are some examples from *Isaac Asimov's Treasury of Humor*:

I am firm; you are stubborn; he's an obstinate mule.
I am liberal; you are radical; she's an extremist.
I am prudent; you are conservative; she's an extremist.
I am far-seeing; you are a visionary; he's a fuzzy-minded dreamer.

Take time to make up your own three statements. Or make up the first statement and let others finish the other two parts.

Transition: Sometimes we give ourselves the benefit of the doubt that we don't give to others, or we see the worst in others and the best in ourselves. Ezekiel wants the people to put themselves into God's story so they can see the worst—and best—in themselves.

Option B: Begin by singing together or playing a recording of "Where Have All the Flowers Gone?" This song by folksinger Pete Seeger is available in many different versions performed by different recording artists.

Transition: The song "Where Have All the Flowers Gone?" tells the story of human folly that repeats the mistakes of the past over and over. Ezekiel tells the cyclical story of Israelite history and assures people that, despite their folly, God is with them.

Engage the Text (20 minutes)
Option A: Listen as someone reads Ezekiel 12:21-23 and writes the old and the new proverbs on newsprint or a chalkboard. It felt to Israelites that God was no longer acting in the world and that the period in which God's saving acts were recorded as scripture was over. But Ezekiel said,

"The days are near, and the fulfillment of every vision." Discuss the following questions.
1. What evidence do we have in scripture or in the movement of the Holy Spirit that every vision will be fulfilled soon?
2. What does "soon" mean?
3. What do you think the vision was?
4. Is the biblical story finished, or is it still an open-ended story?
5. What has not been said in scripture that needs to be said? Anything?
6. How well or how poorly do you relate to the ancient stories in the Bible? How relevant are the stories to your life today?

Option B: Listen as someone reads Ezekiel 20:1-44. This passage recounts the story of the Hebrews in the wilderness after the exodus and compares it to the period of exile and, later, the period of persecution under Antiochus IV Epiphanes. Recall from memory, if you can, other Old Testament stories of sin and grumbling, such as the story of Adam and Eve in the garden, Noah, the Tower of Babel, Israel's request for a king (1 Sam. 8), and David's indiscretion (2 Sam. 11).

List in chronological order on newsprint the lessons God intended the people to learn in each case. What pattern do you see in God's relationship to the people in the overall biblical story? Does the pattern change with the new covenant in Jesus Christ? If so, how? What does Jesus mean when he says, "Go your way, and from now on do not sin again" (John 8:11). Can we break the pattern?

Option C: On newsprint, quickly list the events in sequence from the story of Daniel in the Lion's Den, based on memory or by scanning the story in Daniel 6. Take the roles of Daniel, Darius, the king's advisors, snitches, the faithful who support Daniel, angels, and the lion keepers. Some may wish to be lions. Then act out the story of Daniel and the Lion's Den. Afterwards, reflect on these questions.
1. What are the lessons in this story?
2. In our own workplaces, what happens when a new "king" takes the throne?
3. When have you been delivered from injustice when you least expected it? In your experience who has brought deliverance for the faithful?
4. Who do you know who, like Daniel, is a light to the nations? Whose actions or words are making a difference in your community, your congregation, the world?

Option D: Use these general questions for group discussion about the Bible stories.
1. When have you listened to the accusations of others about another, acted on them, and discovered later they were false?
2. When have you been part of racism in attitude, act, and word? When have you ignored the racist attitudes, acts, and words of others?
3. Reflect on times at work or in other situations when you may have remained silent while another person was thrown to the wolves.
4. Share those times when the law worked against you even when you were right. What similarities and differences do you find in your shared experiences?

Respond (10 MINUTES)

Option A: The people in Ezekiel's time thought the prophecies they were hearing might be for someone else or for another time, or they thought that God had stopped speaking to the people altogether. Use these questions to discuss God's presence with or distance from us today.
1. When have you felt that God was distant and had nothing to say to you?
2. How do you think God reminds powerful leaders today who is truly Lord?
3. There may be times when we need to shed the past, especially if knowledge of the past prevents growth. Reflect on times the church or your life has been hindered by lingering memories of what happened in the past.
4. On the other hand, what lessons from the past do we need to carry with us?
5. Share tips with each other for staying hopeful and maintaining a vision for the future.

Option B: Brainstorm an act of faithfulness that you could do as a group that will, in a nonconfrontive fashion, provide a witness to the power of God in today's world, such as mentoring young people, volunteering for a work camp, or sponsoring a fundraiser to stop hunger. How would you publicize the event without seeming overly pious? Carry out the entire plan.

Option C: Listen as someone reads aloud "The Last Flower" by James Thurber, available from your library in one of his several collections. If possible, pass the book around and allow several people to read. Close this portion with silent reflection. Consider not whether other people ever learn from the past, but whether you yourself can learn from the past.

Session 5

Option D: If you polled your friends, family, and co-workers this week about their hopes and visions, share them now. Then tell what mistakes you have made in your life that you will not repeat. Also, talk about whether children can learn to avoid the mistakes their parents made.

Closing (5 MINUTES)
Sing "Amazing grace" as a group, pausing between each stanza for silent and spoken sentence prayers as each person feels led.

PART III: LEADER GUIDELINES

Items Needed
Bibles
"The Last Flower" by James Thurber
An audio recording of "Where Have All the Flowers Gone?" by Pete Seeger
Chalkboard or newsprint and markers

Tips for Leading
1. Some options use songs and stories that are easy to find in a public library. Be sure to read all the options ahead of time and gather the resources you will need to lead participants through the exercises.
2. Each time you meet, begin by reviewing what happened in the last session before moving on. This will help people who attend infrequently follow the conversation and join in the discussion.
3. Always allow time during Engage the Text to let people ask questions about what is happening in the Bible story. Don't feel that you have to be able to answer each question. Bring a one-volume Bible commentary or books about the prophets to the sessions for handy reference. Invite others in the group to respond to questions if they wish. Share the leadership!
4. Consider bringing in a child's version of the story of Daniel in the Lion's Den. With the group, compare this very simple treatment of the story with the adult version in the Bible. Talk with the group about whether these Bible stories are appropriate for children. What are the lessons children learn from them? What do adults learn?

Session 6
Apocalypse and the Future

Part I: Preparation

Bible passages: Ezekiel 37; Daniel 12

Key verse: At that time Michael, the great prince, the protector of your people, shall arise. There shall be a time of anguish, such as has never occurred since nations first came into existence. But at that time your people shall be delivered, everyone who is found written in the book (Dan. 12:1).

Summary: Ezekiel prophesies that the dry bones in the desert can live again in the end. And God assures the prophet Daniel that the dead will be resurrected in the last days. Those who persevere to be faithful in hard times will live again. Apocalypse is written to God's people under oppression to assure them the troubles of the present won't last forever, but apocalypse also looks ahead to a time when God will put things right, permanently. The end time is not a guessing game. The end time is a radical disjuncture from the present that cannot be predicted—or avoided. How can we live as Christians as if the end times are now? Where are the radical disjunctures from the present in our lives?

Study

The Christian writer C. S. Lewis once pointed out that even though Christians should not follow God for the sake of pie in the sky, it doesn't mean there isn't any. Anyone who reads the Bible from cover to cover will see that other issues, such as justice, overshadow the issue of eternal reward; nevertheless, there are references to God's plan to restore all at the end of time, in a manner of God's choosing. Even though this study debunks the notion that scripture can crack a code to tell us the precise date of the apocalypse, we should not be blind to the fact that these same scriptures very clearly point to a judgment day and vast cosmic events of overarching significance—heaven and hell.

Dry bones

The vision of the dry bones in Ezekiel 37 is one of the most famous and most compelling stories in the Bible. A cemetery can be a peaceful, if somber, place. They are designed, after all, to provide comfort and rest. But the resting place in Ezekiel is another matter. It's a killing field. Few westerners have stood among mounds of human bones, the wind whistling through their hollow dryness, and felt the weight of unholy death and sorrow.

Ezekiel, the representative of a vanquished people, many of whom are dead and many others who are in exile, is taken by the Spirit of the Lord and set down in a valley of dry bones. Ezekiel tells us there are very many bones and they are very dry. When the Lord asks him if these bones might live, Ezekiel seems to be so overwhelmed by the sheer scale of the disaster before him that he can only say, "O Lord God, you know."

> Men of Galilee, why do you stand looking up toward heaven? This Jesus, who has been taken up from you into heaven, will come in the same way as you saw him go into heaven.
>
> Acts 1:11

The real answer that God gives eventually through Ezekiel is, yes, these bones can live. There is nothing that God can't do, of course, and before Ezekiel's eyes the bones rise with a great rattling. Then they are covered with flesh, but they still do not live. They are taking form, but they come to real life only when God breathes the breath of life into them. This is the prophecy that people will be called from their graves.

This is not a mere parlor trick. The point of this resurrection scene is for the people to become God's people again. They are not brought back to life to continue the old way of life, but to pursue a new way of life, God's way of life, which they should have been following all along.

Two other texts from Ezekiel give us some idea of what this new life will be like. Ezekiel 34:23-24 characterizes the coming king, a prince really, as a loving shepherd. This is the classic view of the true king, one who cares for the flock and puts their welfare above all other things. The other, Ezekiel 17:22-24, draws upon another common image from the ancient world—God's community as a great tree. The tree puts down roots into the earth and branches into the sky. The tree provides a home for the creatures of the earth and the birds of the air. The tree provides fruit for sustenance. The strong tree stands fast against the storm. And at the center of the whole kingdom, an ecosystem of sorts, is the true king, drawing in all of creation into one commonwealth. This interconnectedness of the king and all that lives is a central image of God's plan for the people. Taken all together, these images show us a loving, communitarian vision. Now that is a radical disjuncture from the way we're living now.

> They charge. Is Babylon triumphant,
> Her standard raised, her princes grim arrayed,
> With martyrs' trophied skulls ascendant,
> No end in sight their rule of sun and shade?
> Nay. As the waves are spent against the shore,
> They roil and retreat, are seen no more.
>
> —F. Ramirez

More resurrection

The final passage of Daniel, chapter 12, looks ahead to a time of anguish, but also of triumph, for the wise. But who are the "wise" that he refers to in verse 3? And just how many wise people are there? A few? A lot? Is this supposed to be a comfort or a warning?

During the war of the Maccabees, around the year 165 B.C., there were those who took up the sword against the Seleucid Empire, but there were also those, known as "the wise," who revered the stories of Daniel's nonviolent resistance. They, like Daniel, watched and waited for God to work things out in the course of history. To them, fighting against the evil empire was futile and useless. In the end of time, these wise people who endured ". . . shall shine like the brightness of the sky, and those who lead many to righteousness, like the stars forever and ever" (Dan. 12:3).

Daniel quite rightly wants to know, as we all do, when these things will occur. He receives the answer in Daniel 12:7. Things will happen after "a time, two times, and half a time." Later, in 12:12, there is a reference to a "thousand three hundred thirty-five days." The previous verse refers to one thousand two hundred ninety days. It doesn't matter. Biblical numbers are not so much concerned with quantity as quality. And the quality of these times are soon. Seven years in Hebrew thought signified a fulfilled time. By contrast three and a half years, which these various numbers approximate, refers to a broken time, a time cut short, which is precisely what the faithful desire. They want an end to the suffering under the reign of oppression during the second century B.C.

Session 6

Michael shall rise
In the midst of this message, we are introduced to the protector of God's people, the archangel Michael. We are encouraged to learn that we are not alone in this struggle. There are unseen forces; there are angels involved. When things are at their worst, Michael shall rise.

Who are these angels? Why don't we know more about them? How do they work? The word for *angel*, in both Hebrew and Greek, means "messenger." That doesn't tell us much, except perhaps that the purpose of angels is not to prove anything. As near as I can tell from scripture, angels are there to get God's vision done.

Sometimes the angels seem to be God's way of expressing himself. Other times they seem to be beings with their own identities. Their exact nature and purpose is left largely unexplained. There is no systematic "angelology" in the scriptures. But they're there. And it would be as big a mistake to disbelieve in angels as it would be to worship them.

> For what comes is Judgment: happy are those whom it finds labouring in their vocations, whether they were merely going out to feed the pigs or laying good plans to deliver humanity a hundred years hence from some great evil. The curtain has indeed now fallen. Those pigs will never in fact be fed, the great campaign against White Slavery or Governmental Tyranny will never in fact proceed to victory. No matter; you were at your post when the Inspection came.
>
> —C. S. Lewis, "The World's Last Night"

Over a third of a century ago, I was trapped in the confines of my school desk with the rest of Mr. Ever's seventh grade class. It was 9:55 a.m. on a beautiful blue sky day, the sun shining off the mountains that filled the view through our windows. Most of us were thinking that if the world was about to end, the classroom was a foolish place to spend our last minutes, but no one was getting out of his or her chair to lead an exodus.

Some self-described prophet had predicted the world would come to an end at 10:00 a.m., and although none of us fully believed it, at our age we couldn't help but wonder. The minutes counted down. The clock struck the fatal hour, one girl screamed, and we all laughed nervously, glancing out the window.

Nothing happened.

I've been a little skeptical ever since when someone predicts the end of the world…and they did—in 1972, '74, '76, '79, '88, '89, 2000, and so on and so on. The only promise I believe in is God's promise to end the world on God's terms. I mistrust human teachers who may mean well or who manipulate others for their own ends.

Apocalypse and the Future

Apocalyptic literature in the Bible recognizes the fact that the world is made up of two parts—that which is seen and that which is unseen. And the believer knows that the unseen is more powerful than the seen. We labor against the Adversary with full faith in the eventual outcome, knowing God will re-enter history in a dramatic fashion and bring down the curtain on sin's legacy. But we don't really know the details of how this will come to pass.

The message of apocalyptic literature, whether found in Ezekiel, Daniel, Revelation, Zechariah, or the words of Jesus in the Gospels, remains the same from beginning to end. Hold on! God is in control! His will shall be done on earth as it is in heaven.

In God's time.

Things to think about: Examine your lifestyle. Look at your closets, your checkbook register, your schedule, your refrigerator. In what way do these indicate that you are living in a radical disjuncture from the rest of the world? As a family, talk about how you could live more faithfully in God's vision.

Keep a running total of the angels you see this week in stores, in magazines, and on television. Note what they're doing. Comforting? Supporting? Protecting? See if you can find an angel that speaks a challenging word or sends a tough message.

> But let them sleep, Lord, and me mourn a space,
> For, if above all these, my sins abound,
> 'Tis late to ask abundance of thy grace,
> When we are there; here on this lowly ground,
> Teach me how to repent; for that's as good
> As if thou hadst sealed my pardon, with thy blood.
>
> —John Donne, from Holy Sonnet VII

PART II: SESSION

Focus (10 MINUTES)

Greet each other and share announcements. Then choose one of these options to focus on the topic of the session.

Option A: Listen together to a recording of "Dem Bones." After playing it through once, play it again, feeling free to sing along. Get up and dance while you're at it.

Option B: Display a cardboard skeleton, the kind used for a Halloween decoration. As a group, see how many of the bones you can name from memory. Write them on the skeleton or on a sheet of newsprint. As an alternative, take an inventory of broken bones in the group. How many and which bones have been broken over the years in the group? What story goes with each broken bone?

Option C: Pretend that you have all fallen asleep, like Rip Van Winkle, only to awaken twenty-five years in the future. On newsprint write down what you think this future might look like. Post the sheet in a visible place for the remainder of the session.

Transition: Only God can make the dead live again. But it seems unlikely that God would revive us as we are to make the same mistakes again. Ezekiel and Daniel bear a message from God about the promise of new life and how it will be different from our past life.

Engage the Text (20 MINUTES)

Option A: Take a helping of soft modeling clay to shape into bones, laying them in the center of the table or meeting space on a cutting board or newspaper. Keep working during the discussion. When all the clay is used up, study the "field" of bones and try to imagine the scene that Ezekiel saw in the valley.

Talk together about Ezekiel 37, dividing it into two parts: before and after. Focus first on verses 1-14, discussing the following questions. (Look for additional information in a commentary or study Bible.)
1. What do you think the bones represent?
2. How did they get there?
3. Why do the bones feel that hope is lost and they are cut off completely? How did Israel get to be in this horrible state?
4. If God can do anything, even make bones live, why didn't God make Israel be faithful?

Now look at Ezekiel 37:15-28, and discuss the following questions.
1. God restores life to Israel, but it must be different than the life they were living before. In what ways will it be different?
2. What difference does it make that the leader from the line of David will be a prince rather than a king?
3. Is there anything new under the sun? How does the covenant God offers to Israel in Ezekiel 37:26-27 differ from the covenant that God made with Abraham in Genesis 15?
4. Did this new covenant ever happen?

Apocalypse and the Future

Option B: Look at Daniel 12 together. Talk about the following terms. What do they mean?
1. The wise
2. Book
3. The Protector
4. One thousand two hundred ninety days (unfulfilled time)
5. Reward

After clarifying the terms in Daniel 12, work as a whole group, or in small groups, to paraphrase some or all of the chapter. When the paraphrase is finished, listen while someone in the group reads or recites it. What new insights come to you after working with the passage in this way?

Respond (15 MINUTES)

Option A: These passages look to the future, when the people will be restored to God and all battles will be fought by God. Consider together what you hope the future will be like on both sides of the grave. Jot down the characteristics of both. How much alike are they?

For more discussion, use the following questions.
1. How do you view the success of your life? Would you have described it the same way five years ago? ten years ago? What do you hope your future holds?
2. If you understand the truth about something, is there any reason you should keep it a secret as Daniel was told to do? What is it?
3. Has God abandoned us? When does God feel most present? most absent? Where are you in relationship to God? close to God? far away?
4. Have you ever been visited by an angel? Tell about it, if you can.
5. What will the world look like when God's will is done on earth as it is in heaven? How can you bring about at least a little of this in our time?
6. Speak about a great crisis in your life. Were you able to endure until it was over? Were you able to see the end of it at the time?
7. After studying Ezekiel and Daniel, what does apocalypse mean to you now? What have you learned that will be useful in your life?
8. Many believers look to books like Daniel and Ezekiel to provide a detailed road map to the future. What can you say for certain about the future based on apocalyptic literature in the Bible?
9. How dependent is your faith on signs or some sort of visible assurances from God?

Option B: If you know of predictions about the end of the world, share them with the group. Then shift gears. Perhaps it's not necessary to wait for God to enter history in a dramatic way, bringing the world as we know it to an end. What can we do to change the way we live in order to be more faithful? In other words, how can we help to bring a little bit of heaven on earth? And to what extent will we ever be able to achieve such a movement?

Option C: While many apocalypticists view the end of the world as the final judgment, the Bible tells us that the apocalypse will restore the faithful to God and give the world new life. Work together to make a Book of Life for the people in the group to remind yourselves that God is always drawing us in. On a sheet of blank paper, use markers or crayons to write your name and decorate the page. Bind your page with everyone else's in a single binder. Assign someone to make a cover page that says, "Those who are wise shall shine like the brightness of the sky, and those who lead many to righteousness, like the stars forever and ever" (Dan. 12:3). When the book is finished, listen as someone reads it aloud. End with sentence prayers of assurance that we are not alone in our endurance race. Pray aloud if you feel led.

Closing (1 MINUTE)

Pray in unison: Dear God of History, God of the Future, the Past, and the Present, we recognize you as the one in charge of our lives. Where others might despair, we have hope. Where others panic, we are calm. When others might point to the sky, we point to your plan. Where others might choose to hide from the world, we seek to serve you in the world. Bless us as we continue to seek your wisdom in your holy word. We pray these things in the name of Christ. Amen.

PART III: LEADER GUIDELINES

Items Needed
Bibles
Chalkboard or newsprint and markers
Paper and crayons or markers
Binder
Audio recording of "Dem Bones" and tape or CD player
Halloween skeleton
Modeling clay

Apocalypse and the Future

Tips for Leading

1. Like children, adults learn by various methods. Some like to listen and discuss. Others learn best by visualizing something, or role playing, for instance. A variety of options are provided in this session. Try to gauge what works best for the people in the group and plan accordingly.
2. Read about these passages in a Bible commentary before meeting with the group. Spend time this week reflecting on the meaning of these books for yourself. Share your understanding with the group, but be open to hearing what the apocalyptic literature in the Bible means to others. Do not discount anyone's understanding.
3. Review the first session in the unit and refresh your memory on the definition of apocalypse. Remind the group that apocalypse is not about judgment as much as it is about the restoration of God's people to the covenant.
4. Take a few minutes at the end of the session to evaluate this study on Ezekiel and Daniel. Then talk together about the next study you will undertake.